YVETTE CHILDS

25 SPREADSHEET TRIVIA FACTS WITH HOW-TOS

A Collection of Trivia Fun Facts & How-Tos for Spreadsheet Lovers

First edition

This book was professionally typeset on Reedsy.
Find out more at reedsy.com

Contents

Welcome!

Do you love working with spreadsheets? Does it give you a sense of calm when you see everything nicely lined up in rows & columns? Do you see the beauty in graphs? Do you feel a great sense of accomplishment when a formula works the way you want it to? I think that way too.

This bite-sized collection of spreadsheet facts, trivia, and how-tos is designed to be entertaining, informative, and useful. It is not designed to exactly test your skills. Some of the answer choices may be a bit silly, all in good fun. This book is a way to celebrate you and the fact that you love spreadsheets. Let's have a little fun.

"Spreadsheets are a powerful tool for organizing, analyzing, and presenting data. They can help you make sense of complex information and make better decisions."

-Bill Gates-

Chapter 1: How To Use This Book

We'll start with some facts and the history of spreadsheets. You can skip this section and go straight to the trivia if you choose. Each trivia question is either true/false or has 4 multiple-choice options. Only one option is the **most** correct. The answers are in the Answers section after the trivia section. After the answers section, you will find a how-to section inspired by the trivia questions.

Important Information

1. The trivia and information in this book will have a focus on Excel and/or Google Sheets. The questions won't specify which tool. Your challenge is to know or find out the difference if there is one.
2. The information and trivia pertain to spreadsheet usage on a PC, not MAC.
3. I'm aware that there are tons of ways to do a thing in a spreadsheet. The how-tos in this book are based on <u>a</u> way. Your way might be different.
4. I'm aware that naming conventions can be different. I'll be using terms that have been used most frequently based

on my experience. For example, the top section of the spreadsheet in Excel is called the "ribbon". In this book, I will use the word "menu".

Suggested Uses for Fun

- Use it to quiz a lunchtime work friend.
- Use it to quiz your teenager.
- Use it to quiz a family member.
- Use it for a laugh with another spreadsheet enthusiast.
- Use the how-tos to practice your skills.

Chapter 2: Spreadsheet Facts

Definition of a Spreadsheet

Encyclopedia Britannica defines a spreadsheet as a computer program that represents information in a two-dimensional grid of data, along with formulas that relate the data. Historically, a spreadsheet was an accounting ledger that showed various numerical information useful for managing a business. Electronic spreadsheets replaced pen-and-ink versions between 1970 - 1999.

Why It's Called a Spreadsheet

A spreadsheet was a ledger book full of huge **sheets** of paper that would quite literally **spread** across the table. Rows and columns divided these sheets for manually entering data using a pen or pencil.

Timeline of the Spreadsheet

- 1978/79 VisiCalc - Apple II
- 1982 Multiplan - Microsoft
- 1983 Lotus 1-2-3 - IBM
- 1987 Excel - Microsoft
- 2001 Open Office Calc - Apache Software Foundation
- 2006 Google Sheets - Google
- 2007 Numbers - Apple
- 2012 Airtable
- 2016 Notion
- 2019 Coda
- 2019 Causal

Daniel Bricklin and Bob Frankston created the first spreadsheet application in 1978, named VisiCalc for "visible calculator." It was popular on the Apple II, one of the first computers used by businesses.

Lotus 1-2-3 surpassed VisiCalc to become the program that cemented the IBM PC as the preeminent PC in business during the 1980s and 1990s. IBM acquired Lotus in 1995 and continued selling Lotus 1-2-3 through 2013 when it discontinued the spreadsheet application, which had fallen behind Microsoft Excel in the 1990s and never recovered.

While Lotus 1-2-3 was the first to introduce cell names and macros, Microsoft Excel spreadsheets implemented a graphical user interface and the ability to point and click using a mouse.

Spreadsheets for Personal Computers

With the introduction of the graphical user interface (GUI), handling programs such as spreadsheets became user-friendly. Visual components replaced the text-dominated features across the entire software. This completely transformed the nature of the spreadsheet and exponentially increased its use among home users.

Excel 1.0 was the very first GUI-based spreadsheet program that Microsoft specifically built for Macintosh. Later on, they transitioned Excel to the Windows environment, and there was no looking back. Since then, Microsoft Excel has been the most dominant spreadsheet software over the last two decades.

Spreadsheets have come a long way over the past few decades, and they are continuing to become more intuitive, flexible, and powerful than ever. Cloud-based spreadsheets are now a key part of many organizations. Google Sheets offers the most popular free cloud-based spreadsheet program that now ranks number 2 in the world, just behind Microsoft's Excel. This has revolutionized the way businesses can work, allowing collaboration anywhere, and increasing productivity for many.

Chapter 3: Spreadsheet Trivia

The Spreadsheet Menu

1) Why would you want to hide the spreadsheet menu?
   a) You don't like the way it is looking at you.
   b) To give you more real estate on your worksheet.
   c) It serves no purpose.
   d) To keep it safe from harm.

2) What is the benefit of customizing the Quick Access Toolbar?
   a) To quickly access commands you use most frequently.
   b) Wait, you can customize that!?
   c) So you don't have to use the larger menu.
   d) It provides a faster way to open Google Docs.

3) Under which menu option would you find Protect Sheet and Protect Workbook?
   a) Under Data since you are protecting the data.
   b) Under Add-ins since you are adding in protection.
   c) Under Review because that is the intuitive logical place.
   d) Under Insert because you are inserting protection to cells.

4) The formula bar, identified with an fx, is also part of the spreadsheet menu.
   a) True
   b) False

5) Under which menu option would you find "Filter"?
   a) Under View because you want to view a certain set of data.
   b) Under Tools, because you use filters as a tool to view a certain set of data.
   c) Just hide the rows or columns instead of filtering.
   d) Under Data because you are filtering the data.

Sheets / Tabs

1) How do you add another Sheet?
   a) Right-click > Paste Special > Sheet.
   b) Use a sum formula.
   c) Click on the "+" sign located at the bottom near where you see "Sheet1".
   d) Go to File in the menu then select Open

2) What is the benefit of color coding your sheets?
   a) To make them pretty.
   b)So you don't have to name them.
   c)To help visually organize related or like sheet content.
   d) To match company branding guidelines.

3) How do you rename a sheet?

   a) Double-click on the existing name.

   b) Go to File in the menu then select Save as.

   c) Go to Format or Page Layout in the menu. There must be an option under there.

   d) In the formula bar, type "=name".

4) How do you delete a sheet?

   a) Close the spreadsheet without saving it.

   b) Highlight all of the cells then press the delete key on your keyboard.

   c) Right-click on the sheet and select delete.

   d) Right-click on the sheet and select hide. It will eventually delete itself.

5) What is the purpose of grouping sheets?

   a) So they won't be lonely.

   b) To enter the same information or formatting in the same cell(s) on multiple sheets.

   c) Wait, you can group sheets?!

   d) There isn't a need to have the same information or formatting on multiple sheets.

Formatting

1) These are All things that you can format; cells, text, numbers, shapes, pictures.

   a) True

   b) False

2) Under which menu option would you find conditional formatting?
  a) Data because you are formatting data.
  b) File to save the data in a particular format.
  c) Home or Format.
  d) Insert because you are inserting a conditional format.

3) What is Conditional Formatting?
  a) A way to create a rule that will apply a format to cells that meet the rule's criteria.
  b) A way to save the spreadsheet file in a specified format.
  c) A way of setting up a password as the condition for opening the workbook.
  d) A way to create a table.

4) Can you use a formula to format cells?
  a) True
  b) False

5) How can you copy a format from one cell to another?
  a) Use the formula =formatcells.
  b) Press Ctrl + F on your keyboard.
  c) Use the format painter. It is usually identified as a paintbrush icon.
  d) Use the options under the View menu section.

Charts and Graphs

1) Under which menu section would you find the option to insert a column or bar chart?
   a) Add-ins because you are adding in a chart.
   b) Page Layout because you are laying out a chart on the page.
   c) Draw so you can use your mouse to draw the chart.
   d) Insert because you are inserting a chart.

2) What is the benefit of visualizing data in charts and graphs?
   a) They are fun to do.
   b) To fill up the page.
   c) Visualizations help us see trends and patterns in the data to make better sense of it.
   d) Why not. You have plenty of time in your day.

3) What is a Sparkline?
   a) Mr. Spark designed the line graph so they are now named after him.
   b) A mini chart, usually a line or bar, within one cell that quickly shows a trend.
   c) That star-like-looking shape. It may also be called a star or sunburst.
   d) There is no such thing.

4) A combo chart can allow...
   a) A bar chart and a line chart in the same visual.
   b) A user to combine two worksheets.
   c) Two or more combinations of font types.
   d) The ability to graph numbers written as text; Five, Ten, Fifteen, etc.

5) Pie charts are bad so spreadsheet tools no longer have them available?
   a) True
   b) False

Formulas and Functions

1) What is the difference between Vlookup and Hlookup?
   a) There is no difference.
   b) Use Index with Match instead.
   c) Vlookup is a vertical lookup, Hlookup for horizontal lookup.
   d) Vlookup is value lookup while Hlookup is histogram lookup.

2) What function is used to evaluate if a formula resulted in an error?
   a) LOOKUP will lookup errors.
   b) ISERROR evaluates the result returning TRUE if there is an error, FALSE if no error.
   c) SEARCH searches for errors.
   d) FIND will find errors.

3) What is the purpose of an "IF" statement?
   a) Is a logic statement that performs one action if the condition is true another if false.
   b) To determine if you should use one function or another.
   c) It is placed at the end of an AS function "ASIF".
   d) Helps you decide if you want to work today or not.

4) This is a valid formula =**IF(SUM(A1:A20)>100,"Y","N")**
   a) True
   b) False

5) Is it better to add values by using auto-sum, the sum formula or manually selecting a value, typing "+" and selecting another value?
   a) The sum formula is best.
   b) The auto-sum feature is best.
   c) Manually selecting values and entering "+" is best.
   d) It does not matter, do what you feel comfortable with, just don't use a calculator.

Chapter 4: Answers

The Spreadsheet Menu

1) Why would you want to hide the spreadsheet menu?
   b. To give you more real estate on your worksheet.

2) What is the benefit of customizing the Quick Access Toolbar?
   a. To quickly access commands you use most frequently.

3) Under which menu option would you find Protect Sheet and Protect Workbook?
   c. Under Review because that is the intuitive logical place.

4) The formula bar, identified with an fx, is also part of the spreadsheet menu.
   b. False- it serves a separate purpose as a place to view and edit formulas.

5) Under which menu option would you find "filter"?
   d. Under Data because you are filtering the data.

Sheets / Tabs

1) How do you add another Sheet?

   c. Click on the "+" sign located at the bottom near where you see "Sheet1"

2) What is the benefit of color coding your sheets

   c. To help visually organize related or like sheet content. (a. b. Or d. are also acceptable)

3) How do you rename a sheet?

   a. Double-click on the existing name.

4) How do you delete a sheet?

   c. Right-click on the sheet and select delete. (a. if you add a sheet without saving)

5) What is the purpose of grouping sheets?

   b. To enter the same information or duplicate formatting in the same cell(s) on multiple sheets at a time.

Formatting

1) These are All things that you can format in some manner: cells, text, numbers, shapes, pictures.

   a. True - You can change colors, size, shading, number style, and more.

2) Under which menu option would you find conditional formatting?

c. Home or Format - Home in Excel, Format in Google Sheets

3) What is Conditional Formatting?

a. A way to create a rule that will apply a format to cells that meet the rule's criteria.

4) Can you use a formula to format cells, text, and numbers somehow?

a. True - This option can be found under conditional formatting.

5) How can you copy a format from one cell to another?

c. Use the format painter. It is usually identified as a paintbrush icon.

Charts and Graphs

1) Under which menu section would you find the option to insert a column or bar chart?

d. Insert because you are inserting a chart.

2) What is the benefit of visualizing data in charts and graphs?

c. Visualizations help us see trends and patterns in the data to make better sense of it.

3) What is a Sparkline?

b. A mini chart, usually a line or bar, within one cell that quickly shows a trend.

4) A combo chart can allow...
a. A bar chart and a line chart in the same visual.

5) Pie charts are bad so spreadsheet tools no longer have them available?
b. False - I have found that report stakeholders (especially in Marketing) like pie graphs

Formulas and Functions

1) What is the difference between Vlookup and Hlookup?
c. Vlookup is a vertical lookup where your data is organized vertically. Hlookup is a horizontal lookup where your data is organized horizontally.

2) What function is used to evaluate if a formula resulted in an error?
b. ISERROR evaluates the result returning TRUE if there is an error, and FALSE if there is no error.

3) What is the purpose of an "IF" statement?
a. It is a logic statement that will perform one action if the condition is true and another action if false

4) his is a valid formula =IF(SUM(A1:A20)>100,"Y","N")
a. True - This formula will return a "Y" if the resulting sum is >100 and a "N" if not.

5) Is it better to add values by using auto-sum, the sum formula or manually selecting a value, typing "+" and selecting another value?

d. It does not matter, do what you feel most comfortable with, just don't pull out the calculator

Chapter 5: How-Tos

How-To Hide the Menu Bar

Google Sheets

1. Click the arrow or carrot button in the top right corner of your screen.

Excel

1. Right-click on any ribbon/menu tab and select Collapse the Ribbon

Or

1. Click the boxed arrow next to the minimize button in the top right corner of your screen and select what option you want.

How-To Customize the Quick Access Toolbar

Excel

1. Click the down arrow at the right end of the Quick Access Toolbar.
2. Select More Commands
3. In the Choose commands from the drop-down list, select All Commands.
4. Select the commands you want to add to the Quick Access Toolbar and click the Add button.
5. To remove a command from the Quick Access Toolbar, select it and click the Remove button.
6. To rearrange the order of the commands on the Quick Access Toolbar, select a command and click the Move Up or Move Down button.
7. Click OK to save your changes.

How-To Protect a Sheet

Google Sheets

1. Click the "Data" tab in the menu bar.
2. Select Protect sheets & ranges
3. Select Add a sheet or range
4. Select the Sheet option
5. Use the pull-down to select the sheet you want to protect
6. Click Set permissions and select the Range editing permissions option you want

7. Click the "Done" button to save your changes.

To unprotect

1. Select the sheet you want to unprotect.
2. Click the Data tab in the menu bar.
3. Click Protect sheets and ranges.
4. Select the sheet you want to unprotect.
5. Click on the trash can.
6. Click the Remove button.
7. Click the OK button

Excel

1. Click the Review tab in the ribbon.
2. In the Protect group, click the Protect Sheet button.
3. In the Protect Sheet dialog box, enter a password in the Password to unprotect sheet box. Leave blank if you don't want a password. IMPORTANT: if you forget the password you will not be able to unprotect the sheet.
4. Confirm the password by entering it again in the Confirm password box.
5. Select the permissions you want to allow users to have on the protected sheet.
6. Click the "OK" button to protect the sheet.

To unprotect

1. Click the Review tab in the ribbon.
2. In the Protect group, click the Unprotect Sheet button.
3. If prompted, enter the password for the sheet.

How-To Apply a Filter

Google Sheets

1. Select the range of cells you want to filter.
2. Click the Data menu and select create filter view.
3. A filter icon will appear next to each column header.
4. Click the filter icon for the column you want to filter.
5. Select the values you want to show in the filtered view.
6. Click OK to apply the filter.

Excel

1. Select the range of cells you want to filter.
2. Click the Data tab in the ribbon.
3. Click the Filter button in the Sort & Filter group.
4. A drop-down arrow will appear in each column header.
5. Click the drop-down arrow for the column you want to filter.
6. Select the values you want to filter by.
7. Click OK to apply the filter.

How-To Group Sheets

Excel

1. Select the sheets you want to group. To select multiple sheets, hold down the Ctrl key while clicking on each sheet's tab or Shift key if the sheets are next to each other.
2. Click on any one sheet to un-group.

How-To Apply Conditional Formatting

Google Sheets

1. Select the cells you want to format.
2. Click the Format menu and select Conditional formatting.
3. In the Conditional formatting sidebar, select single color.
4. In the Format cells if section, select the condition you want to apply.
5. In the Format style section, select the formatting you want to apply to the cells that meet the condition.
6. Click the Done button to save your changes.

Excel

1. Select the range of cells you want to format.
2. Click the Home tab in the ribbon.
3. In the Styles group, click the Conditional Formatting button.
4. Select the rule you want to apply.

5. Specify the formatting you want to apply to the cells that meet the condition.
6. Click the OK button to apply the rule.

How-To Use a Formula to Apply Formatting

Excel - This is a feature within conditional formatting. This example refers to formatting one cell based on a formula.

1. Select the cell you want to format.
2. Click the Home tab in the ribbon.
3. In the Styles group, click the Conditional Formatting button.
4. Select New Rule.
5. Under Select a Rule Type, select Use a formula to determine which cells to format.
6. Enter a formula. Example = A1 > B1
7. Click the Format button and specify the formatting you want to apply to the cell if it meets the formula's condition. Click the OK button.
8. Click the next OK button to apply the rule.

How-To Insert Charts and Graphs

Google Sheets

1. Select the data you want to chart.
2. Click the Insert menu and select Chart.
3. In the Insert Chart dialog box, select the type of chart you want to create.
4. Click the Create button.
5. Google Sheets may automatically generate the chart based on the selected data.
6. The chart will be inserted into your spreadsheet.
7. You can customize the chart by clicking on it and selecting the three dots in the right corner to open the Chart editor.

Excel

1. Select the data you want to chart.
2. Click the Insert tab in the ribbon.
3. In the Charts group, click the type of chart you want to insert.
4. A chart will be inserted into your worksheet.
5. To customize the chart, select the chart and click the Chart Design tab in the ribbon.
6. Use the options in the Chart Design tab to change the chart's layout, colors, and other formatting options.

How-To Insert a Sparkline

Google Sheets

1. Put your cursor in the cell where you want the sparkline
2. Click the Insert tab
3. Hover over Functions
4. Hover over Google
5. Select SPARKLINE
6. Enter or select the cell range you want
7. Press Enter
8. The sparkline will be inserted into the selected cell

Excel

1. Select the cell where you want to insert the sparkline.
2. Click the Insert tab in the ribbon.
3. In the Sparklines group, select the type of sparkline you want to insert.
4. Select the range of data you want to include in the sparkline.
5. Click OK to insert the sparkline.

How-To Use Vlookup and Hlookup

Google Sheets and Excel

VLOOKUP and HLOOKUP are two powerful functions that allow you to look up data in a table or range of cells and return a corresponding value.

VLOOKUP

VLOOKUP stands for vertical lookup and is used to search for data in a table or range of cells arranged in rows and columns. The syntax for VLOOKUP is as follows:

=VLOOKUP(lookup_value, table_array, col_index, [range_lookup])

- **lookup_value:** The value you want to look up in the table.
- **table_array:** The range of cells that contains the data you want to search.
- **col_index:** The column number in the table_array that contains the value you want to return.
- **range_lookup:** An optional parameter that specifies whether you want an exact match or an approximate match. The default value is TRUE, which means that an exact match is required.

HLOOKUP

HLOOKUP stands for horizontal lookup and is used to search for data in a table or range of cells arranged in rows and columns. The syntax for HLOOKUP is as follows:

=HLOOKUP(lookup_value, table_array, row_index, [range_lookup])

- **lookup_value:** The value you want to look up in the table.
- **table_array:** The range of cells that contains the data you want to search.
- **row_index:** The row number in the table_array that contains the value you want to return.
- **range_lookup:** An optional parameter that specifies whether you want an exact match or an approximate match. The default value is TRUE, which means that an exact match is required.

Examples

=VLOOKUP(E2, A2:C8, 3, FALSE)
=HLOOKUP(B8, B1:H3, 3, FALSE)

How-To Use an ISERROR Function

Google Sheets and Excel

1. Click on the cell where you want to enter the ISERROR function.
2. Type the following formula into the cell:

=ISERROR(cell_reference)

where cell_reference is the cell you want to check for an error value. For example, if you want to check if cell A1 contains an error value, you would enter the following formula:

=ISERROR(A1)

1. Press Enter.

The ISERROR function will return TRUE if cell A1 contains an error value, or FALSE if it does not.

How To Use an IF Function

Google Sheets and Excel

=IF(logical_test, value_if_true, value_if_false)
Where:

- **logical_test** is the condition you want to test.
- **value_if_true** is the value you want to return if the condition is true.
- **value_if_false** is the value you want to return if the condition is false.

For example, the following formula returns "Yes" if the value in cell A1 is greater than 10, and "No" if it is not.
=IF(A1>10, "Yes", "No")

Thank You

I understand that countless books are vying for your attention, and the fact that you chose mine is an honor. Thanks for reading and playing along! I hope you found this book both fun and informative.

I'd appreciate it if you submitted your feedback on Amazon. Whether it's praise, criticism, or simply your thoughts on the book, I welcome it with open arms. Your insights are invaluable to me as I grow and develop as a writer. Thank you again.

Resources

Frederick. (2023b, April 10). *The History Of Spreadsheets, from VisiCalc to Causal & beyond.* Call Me Fred. https://callmefred.co m/the-history-of-spreadsheets/#google_vignette

The Editors of Encyclopedia Britannica. (2025, January 17). *Spreadsheet | Definition, Uses, & Facts.* Encyclopedia Britannica. https://www.britannica.com/technology/spreadsheet

Meikle, H. (2023, September 8). The history of spreadsheets - Sheetgo Blog. *Sheetgo Blog.* https://blog.sheetgo.com/spreadsh eets-tips/history-of-spreadsheets/

Kirvan, P., & Hanna, K. T. (2024, November 19). *What are spreadsheets and how do they work?* WhatIs. https://www.te chtarget.com/whatis/definition/spreadsheet